SAYINGS
OF
BUDDHA

ILLUSTRATED WITH

WOOD-ENGRAVINGS BY

BOYD HANNA FOR THE

PETER PAUPER PRESS

MT. VERNON · NEW YORK

FOREWORD

ACCORDING to legend the man who became Buddha, or the Enlightened One, was born a prince, over five hundred years before Christ. He was screened by a doting father from all unhappiness until he was married, and himself a father. Then, accidentally, he learned about old age, sickness, and death, and suddenly it was clear to him that he had been depending on transient things for his happiness. He stole away from his home to seek a truth which would not decay, and after a long asceticism which brought him no help, the truth he sought was revealed under the Bodhi-tree. He became the Buddha, the Enlightened One. He began to explain the Dharma, or Truth. Through many years he preached the Eightfold Path, and the brotherhood of Buddhist monks grew in size and influence. Upon his death his disciples (according to legend) recorded his sayings for the sake of future generations.

But it is not certain that the earliest Buddhist books date back twenty-five hundred years to his death. The narrative of his life has as its principal source the Sanskrit stories of the monk

the 8-fold path does not include reincarnation check it out !?

Asvaghosha, which were translated into Chinese in 420 A.D. and from the Chinese into English by Samuel Beale in the Eighteenth Century.

The present text is derived chiefly from *The Gospel of Buddha*, a compilation by Paul Carus from many source-books of Buddhist teachings, including Beale.

The picture of Buddha that comes down to us from these sources is that of a sage, who in his understanding wisdom is able to open up in other men's minds a revelation of the nature of life. He is not a god or a man carrying from Heaven a supernatural revelation, to be accepted on faith. He does not speak of a God, a Creator. He does not tell *why* we live, but *how* to live. He teaches a way of life, a way to rise above the troubles of life, and finally a way to achieve the ultimate happiness of Nirvana, in which state of blissful non-being untroubled peace is combined with the complete opening-up of understanding.

The reward for such a way of life promises immortality only in the disciple's awareness of his identity with the immortal process, a process in which he is the product of earlier lives' thoughts and deeds (karma), and in turn continues the life-stream by present thoughts and deeds which will flow into future lives.

reincarnation worked in later?

SAYINGS OF
BUDDHA

I HAVE RECOGNIZED the deepest truth, which is sublime and peace-giving, but difficult to understand; for most men move in a sphere of worldly interests and find their delight in worldly desires. The worldling will not understand the doctrine, for to him there is happiness in selfhood only, and the bliss that lies in a complete surrender to truth is unintelligible to him. He will call resignation what to the enlightened mind is the purest joy. He will see annihilation where the perfected one finds immortality. He will regard as death what the conqueror of self knows to be life everlasting. The truth remains hidden from him who is in the bondage of hate and desire. Nirvana remains incomprehensible to the vulgar whose minds are beclouded with worldly interests.

❦ The Tathagata [Perfect One] does not seek salvation in austerities, but neither does he for that reason indulge in worldly pleasures, nor live in abundance. He has found the middle path.

Neither abstinence from fish and flesh, nor going naked, nor shaving the head, nor wearing matted hair, nor dressing in a rough garment, nor covering oneself with dirt, nor sacrificing to Agni, will cleanse a man who is not free from delusions. Anger, drunkenness, obstinacy, big-

7

otry, deception, envy, self-praise, disparagement, superciliousness and evil intentions constitute uncleanness; not verily the eating of flesh.

And sensuality is enervating. The self-indulgent man is a slave to his passions, and pleasure-seeking is degrading and vulgar. But to satisfy the necessities of life is not evil. To keep the body in good health is a duty, for otherwise we shall not be able to trim the lamp of wisdom, and keep our minds strong and clear. Water surrounds the lotus, but does not wet its petals. This is the middle path that keeps aloof from both extremes.

The spokes of the wheel are the rules of pure conduct: justice is the uniformity of their length; wisdom is the tire; modesty and thoughtfulness are the hub in which the immovable axle of truth is fixed. He who recognizes the existence of suffering, its cause, its remedy, and its cessation has fathomed the four noble truths. He will walk in the right path. Right views will be the torch to light his way. Right aspirations will be his guide. Right speech will be his dwelling-place on the road. His gait will be straight, for it is right behavior. His refreshments will be the right way of earning his livelihood. Right efforts will be his steps: right thoughts his breath; and right contemplation will give him the peace that follows.

🌿 Now, this is the noble truth concerning suffering: Birth comes with pain, decay is painful, disease is painful, death is painful. Union with the unpleasant is painful, painful is separation from the pleasant; and any craving that is unsatisfied, that too is painful. In brief, bodily conditions which spring from attachment are painful. This is the noble truth concerning suffering.

Now this is the noble truth concerning the origin of suffering: Verily, it is that craving which causes the renewal of existence, accompanied by sensual delight, seeking satisfaction now here, now there, the craving for the gratification of the passions, the craving for a future life, and the craving for happiness in this life. This is the noble truth concerning the origin of suffering.

Now this is the noble truth concerning the destruction of suffering. Verily, it is the destruction, in which no passion remains, of this very thirst! it is the laying aside of, the being free from, this thirst. This is the noble truth concerning the destruction of suffering.

Now, this is the noble truth concerning the way which leads to the destruction of sorrow: Verily! it is this noble eightfold path; that is to say: Right views; right aspirations; right speech; right behavior; right livelihood; right effort; right thoughts; right contemplation. This is the noble truth concerning the destruction of sorrow.

✄ He who knows the nature of self and understands how the senses act, finds no room for selfishness, and thus he will attain peace unending. The world holds the thoughts of self, and from this arises false apprehension. Some say that the self endures after death, some say it perishes. Both are wrong and their error is most grievous. For if the self is perishable, the fruit they strive for will perish too, and at some time there will be for them no hereafter. Good and evil would be indifferent. This salvation from selfishness is without merit.

But if as some on the other hand say, the self will not perish, then in the midst of all life and death there is but one identity unborn and undying. If such is their self, then it is perfect and cannot be perfected by deeds. The lasting, imperishable self could never be changed. The self would be lord and master; moral aims and salvation would be unnecessary.

But we see the marks of joy and sorrow, and say: Where is any constancy? If there is no permanent self that does our deeds, then there is no self; no actor behind our actions, no perceiver behind our perception, no lord behind our deeds.

Now attend and listen: The senses meet the object and from their contact sensation is born. Thence results recollection. Thus, as the sun's power through a burning-glass causes fire to appear, so through the cognizance born of sense and object, the mind originates and with it the ego, the thought of self, whom some Brahman teachers call the lord. The shoot springs from the seed; the seed is not the shoot; both are not one and the same, but successive phases in a continuous growth. Such is the birth of animated life.

He who has found there is no self, will let go all the lusts and desires of egotism. The cleaving to things, covetousness, and sensuality inherited from former existence, are the causes of the misery and vanity in the world. Surrender the grasping disposition of selfishness, and you will attain perfect peace, goodness, and wisdom.

🚩 Gifts are great, the founding of temples is meritorious, meditations and religious exercises pacify the heart, comprehension of the truth leads to Nirvana — but greater than all is loving-kindness. As the light of the moon is sixteen times stronger than the light of all the stars, so is loving-kindness sixteen times more efficacious in liberating the heart than all other religious accomplishments taken together. This state of heart is the best in the world. Let a man remain steadfast in it while he is awake, whether he is standing, walking, sitting, or lying down.

🚩 The charitable man is loved by all; his friend-ship is prized highly; in death his heart is at rest and full of joy, for he suffers not from re-pentance; he receives the opening flower of his reward and the fruit that ripens from it. Hard it is to understand: By giving away food, we get more strength; by bestowing clothing on others, we gain more beauty; by donating abodes of purity and truth, we acquire great treasures.

There is a proper time and a proper mode in charity; just as the vigorous warrior goes to battle, so is the man who is able to give. He is like a warrior, a champion strong and wise in action. Loving and compassionate, he gives with reverence, and banishes all hatred, envy, and anger.

The charitable man has found the path of salvation. He is like the man who plants a sapling, securing thereby the shade, the flowers, and the fruit in future years.

🪶 A kind man who makes good use of wealth is rightly said to possess a great treasure; but the miser who hoards up his riches will have no profit. Charity is rich in returns; charity is the greatest wealth, for though it scatters, it brings no repentance.

🪶 The bliss of a religious life is attainable by every one who walks in the noble eightfold path. He that cleaves to wealth had better cast it away than allow his heart to be poisoned by it; but he who does not cleave to wealth, and possessing riches, uses them rightly, will be a blessing unto his fellows. It is not life and wealth and power that enslave men, but the cleaving to life and wealth and power. The monk who retires from the world in order to lead a life of leisure will have no gain, for a life of indolence is an abomination, and lack of energy is to be despised. The Way of the Teacher does not require a man to go into homelessness or to resign the world, unless he feels called upon to do so; but the Way of the Teacher requires every man to free himself from the illusion of self, to cleanse his heart, to give up his thirst for pleasure, and lead a life of righteousness. And whatever men do, whether they remain in the world as artisans, merchants, and officers of the king, or retire from the world and devote themselves to a life of religious meditation, let them put their whole heart into their task; let them be diligent and energetic, and, if they are like the lotus, which, although it grows in the water, yet remains untouched by the water, if they struggle in life without cherishing envy or hatred, if they live in the world not a life of self but a life of truth, then surely joy, peace, and bliss will dwell in their minds.

🦋 I know that the king's heart is full of love and that for his son's sake he feels deep grief. But let the ties of love that bind him to the son whom he lost embrace with equal kindness all his fellow-beings, and he will receive in his place a greater one than Siddhattha;* he will receive the Buddha, the teacher of truth, and the peace of Nirvana will enter into his heart.

🦋 My son asks for his inheritance. I cannot give him perishable treasures that will bring cares and sorrows, but I can give him the inheritance of a holy life, which is a treasure that will not perish.

....

* Buddha's personal name. This speech is addressed to his father, the following to his son.

Gold and silver and jewels are not in my possession. But if thou art willing to receive spiritual treasures, and art strong enough to carry them and to keep them, I shall give thee the four truths which will teach thee the eightfold path of righteousness. Dost thou desire to be admitted to the brotherhood of those who devote their life to the culture of the heart seeking for the highest bliss attainable?

⚡ Life is instantaneous and living is dying. Just as the chariot-wheel in rolling rolls only at one point of the tire, and in resting rests at one point; in the same way the life of a living being lasts only for the period of one thought. As soon as that thought has ceased the being is said to have ceased.

As to Name and Form, we must understand how they interact. Name has no power of its own, nor can it go on of its own impulse, either to eat, or to drink, or to utter sounds, or to take a movement. Form also is without power and cannot go on of its own impulse. It has no desire to eat, or to drink, or to utter sounds, or to make a movement. But Form goes on when supported by Name, and Name when supported by Form. When Name has a desire to eat, or to drink, or

to utter sounds, or to make a movement, then
Form eats, drinks, utters sounds, moves.

It is as if two men, the one blind from birth
and the other a cripple, were desirous of going
traveling, and the crippled man were to mount on
the shoulders of the blind man and were to direct
him, saying, "Leave the left and go to the right;
leave the right and go to the left."

Here the man blind from birth is without power of his own, and weak, and cannot go of his own impulse or might. The cripple also is without power of his own, and weak, and cannot go of his own impulse or might. Yet when they mutually support one another it is not impossible for them to go. In exactly the same way Name is without power of its own. Form also is without power of its own. Yet when they mutually support one another it is not impossible for them to spring up and go on.

When Name and Form dissolve, they do not exist anywhere, any more than there is heaped-up music material. When a lute is played upon, there is no previous store of sound; and when the music ceases it does not go anywhither in space. It came into existence on account of the structure and stem of the lute and the exertions of the performer; and as it came into existence so it passes away.

In exactly the same way, all the elements of being, both corporeal and non-corporeal, come into existence after having been non-existent; and having come into existence pass away.

There is not a self-residing in Name and Form, but the cooperation of the conformations produces what people call a man. Just as the word "chariot" is but a mode of expression for axle, wheels, the chariot-body and other constituents in their proper combination, so a living being is the appearance of the groups with the four elements as they are joined in a unit. There is no self in the chariot and there is no permanent individual self in man.

Paradoxical though it may seem: There is a path to walk on, there is walking being done, but there is no traveler. There are deeds being done, but there is no doer. There is a blowing of the air, but there is no wind that does the blowing. The thought of self is an error and all existences are as hollow as the plantain tree and as empty as twirling water bubbles.

Therefore as there is no self, there is no transmigration of a self; but there are deeds and the continued effect of deeds. There is a rebirth of karma; there is reincarnation. This rebirth, this reincarnation, this re-appearance of the conformations is continuous and depends on the law of cause and effect. Just as a seal is impressed upon the wax reproducing the configurations of its device, so the thoughts of men, their characters, their aspirations are impressed upon others in continuous transference and continue their karma, and good deeds will continue in blessings while bad deeds will continue in curses.

The body is a compound of perishable organs. It is subject to decay; we should attend to its needs without being attached to it, or loving it. The body is like a machine, and there is no self in it that makes it walk or act, but the thoughts of it, as the windy elements, cause the machine to work. The body moves about like a cart.

✍ Since there is no self, there can not be any after life of a self. Therefore abandon all thought of self. But since there are deeds and since deeds continue, be careful with your deeds. All beings have karma as their portion: they are heirs of their karma; they are sprung from their karma; their karma is their kinsman; their karma is their refuge; karma allots beings to meanness or to greatness.

The rational nature of man is a spark of the true light; it is the first step on the upward road. But new births are required to insure an ascent to the summit of existence, the enlightenment of mind and heart, where the immeasurable light of moral comprehension is gained which is the source of all righteousness. Having attained this higher birth,

I have found the truth and have taught you the
noble path that leads to the city of peace. I have
shown you the way to the lake of ambrosia, which
washes away all evil desire. I have given you the
refreshing drink called the perception of truth,
and he who drinks of it becomes free from excite-
ment, passion, and wrong-doing.

The very gods envy the bliss of him who has escaped from the floods of passion and has climbed the shores of Nirvana. His heart is cleansed from all defilement and free from all illusion. He is like unto the lotus which grows in the water, yet not a drop of water adheres to its petals. The man who walks in the noble path lives in the world, and yet his heart is not defiled by worldly desires.

He who does not see the four noble truths, he who does not understand the three characteristics and has not grounded himself in the uncreate, has still a long path to traverse: by repeated births through the desert of ignorance with its mirages of illusion, and through the morass of wrong. But now that you have gained comprehension, the cause of further migrations and aberrations is removed. The goal is reached. The craving of selfishness is destroyed, and the truth is attained. This is true deliverance; this is salvation; this is heaven and the bliss of a life immortal.

All acts of living become bad by ten things, and by avoiding the ten things they become good. There are three evils of the body, four evils of the tongue, and three evils of the mind.

The evils of the body are, murder, theft, and adultery; of the tongue, lying, slander, abuse, and idle talk; of the mind, covetousness, hatred, and error.

I exhort you to avoid the ten evils: 1. Kill not, but have regard for life. 2. Steal not, and do not rob; but help everybody to be master of the fruits of his labor. 3. Abstain from impurity, and lead a life of chastity. 4. Lie not, be truthful. Speak the truth with discretion, fearlessly and in a loving heart. 5. Invent not evil reports, and do not repeat them. Carp not, but look for the good sides of your fellow-beings, so that you may with sincerity defend them against their enemies. 6. Swear not, but speak decently and with dignity. 7. Waste not the time with gossip, but speak to the purpose or keep silence. 8. Covet not, nor envy, but rejoice at the fortunes of other people. 9. Cleanse your heart of malice and cherish no hatred, not even against your enemies; but embrace all living beings with kindness. 10. Free your mind of ignorance and be anxious to learn the truth, lest you fall a prey either to scepticism or to errors. Scepticism will make you indifferent and errors will lead you astray, so that you shall not find the noble path that leads to life eternal.

What is evil? Killing is evil, stealing is evil, yielding to sexual passion is evil, lying is evil,

23

slandering is evil, abuse is evil, gossip is evil; envy is evil, hatred is evil, to cling to false doctrine is evil; all these things are evil.

And what is the root of evil? Desire is the root of evil, hatred is the root of evil, illusion is the root of evil; these things are the root of evil.

What, however, is good? Abstaining from killing is good, abstaining from theft is good, abstaining from sensuality is good, abstaining from falsehood is good, abstaining from slander is good, suppression of unkindness is good, abandoning gossip is good, letting go all envy is good, dismissing hatred is good, obedience to the truth is good; all these things are good.

And what is the root of the good? Freedom from desire is the root of the good, freedom from hatred and freedom from illusion; these things are the root of the good.

What, however, is suffering? What is the origin of suffering? What is the annihilation of suffering? Birth is suffering, old age is suffering, disease is suffering, death is suffering, sorrow and misery are suffering, affliction and despair are suffering, to be united with loathsome things is suffering, the loss of that which we love and the failure in attaining that which is longed for are suffering; all these things are suffering.

And what is the origin of suffering? It is lust, passion, and the thirst for existence that yearns for pleasure everywhere, leading to a continual rebirth! It is sensuality, desire, selfishness; all these things are the origin of suffering.

And what is the annihilation of suffering? The radical and total annihilation of this thirst and the abandonment, the liberation, the deliverance from passion, that is the annihilation of suffering.

And what is the path that leads to the annihilation of suffering? It is the holy eightfold path that leads to the annihilation of suffering, which consists of right views, right decision, right speech, right action, right living, right struggling, right thoughts, and right meditation.

In so far as a noble youth thus recognizes suffering and the origin of suffering, as he recognizes the annihilation of suffering, and walks on the path that leads to the annihilation of suffering, radically forsaking passion, subduing wrath, annihilating the vain conceit of the "I-am," leaving ignorance, and attaining to enlightenment, he will make an end of all suffering even in this life.

🖋 The Perfect One is like unto a powerful king who rules his kingdom with righteousness, but being attacked by envious enemies goes out to wage war against his foes. When the king sees his soldiers fight he is delighted with their gallantry and will bestow upon them donations of all kinds. You are the soldiers of the Perfect One, while Mara, the Evil One, is the enemy who must be conquered. And the Tathagata will give to his soldiers the city of Nirvana, the great capital of the good law. And when the enemy is overcome the great king of truth will bestow upon all his disciples the most precious crown, which jewel brings perfect enlightenment, supreme wisdom, and undisturbed peace.

✄ The Teacher sees the universe face to face and understands its nature. He proclaims the truth both in its letter and in its spirit, and his doctrine is glorious in its origin, glorious in its progress, glorious in its consummation. The Teacher reveals the higher life in its purity and perfection. He can show you the way to that which is contrary to the five great hindrances. The Teacher lets his mind pervade the four quarters of the world with thoughts of love. And thus the whole wide world, above, below, around, and everywhere will continue to be filled with love, far-reaching, grown great, and beyond measure. Just as a mighty trumpeter makes himself heard — and that without difficulty — in all the four quarters of the earth; even so is the coming of the Teacher: there is not one living creature that the Teacher passes by or leaves aside, but regards them all with mind set free, and deep-felt love.

ॐ *Simha the general said: "I have heard that the Blessed One denies the result of actions; he teaches the doctrine of non-action, saying that actions do not receive their reward, for the Way is the annihilation and the contemptibleness of*

*all things. And teachest thou the doing away of
the soul and the burning away of man's being?
Pray tell me, Lord, do those who speak thus say
the truth?" Buddha replied:*

There is a way, Simha, in which one who says
so, is speaking truly of me; on the other hand,
Simha, there is a way in which one who says the
opposite is speaking truly of me, too. Listen, and
I will tell you: I teach the not-doing of such actions as are unrighteous, either by deed, or by
word, or by thought; I teach the not-bringing-
about of all those conditions of heart which are
evil and not good. However, I teach the doing of
such actions as are righteous, by deed, by word,
and by thought; I teach the bringing about of all
those conditions of heart which are good.

I teach that all the conditions of heart which
are evil and not good, and unrighteous action
by deed, by word, and by thought, must be burnt
away. He who has freed himself from all those
conditions of heart which are evil and not good,
he who has destroyed them as a palm-tree which
is rooted out, so they cannot grow up again, such
a man has accomplished the eradication of self.

I proclaim, Simha, the annihilation of egotism,
of lust, of ill-will, of delusion. However, I do not
proclaim the annihilation of forbearance, of love,

29

of charity, and of truth. I deem unrighteous actions contemptible, whether they be performed by deed, or by word, or by thought; but I deem virtue and righteousness praiseworthy.

🔖 Simha said: "One doubt still lurks in my mind concerning the doctrine of the Blessed One. I am a soldier, and am appointed by the king to enforce his laws and to wage his wars. Does the Tathagata who teaches kindness and compassion permit the punishment of the criminal? Does the Tathagata declare that it is wrong to go to war for the protection of our homes, our wives, our children, and our property? Does the Tathagata teach the doctrine of a complete self-surrender? Does the Tathagata maintain that warfare waged for a righteous cause should be forbidden?" Buddha replied:

He who deserves punishment must be punished, and he who is worthy of favor must be favored. Yet at the same time the Tathagata teaches to do no injury to any living being but to be full of love and kindness. These injunctions are not contradictory, for whosoever must be punished for the crimes which he has committed, suffers his injury not through the ill-will of the judge but on account of his evil-doing. His own acts have brought upon him the injury that the executor of the law inflicts. When a magistrate punishes, let him not harbor hatred in his breast; and a murderer, when put to death, should consider that this is the fruit of his own act.

The Tathagata teaches that all warfare in which man tries to slay his brother is lamentable, but he does not teach that those who go to war in a righteous cause, after having exhausted all means to preserve the peace, are blameworthy. He must be blamed who is the cause of war. The Tathagata teaches a complete surrender of self, but he does not teach a surrender of anything to those powers that are evil, be they men or gods or the elements of nature. Struggle must be, for all life is a struggle of some kind. But he that struggles should look to it lest he struggle in the interest of self against truth and righteousness.

He who struggles in the interest of self, so that he himself may be great or powerful or rich or famous, will have no reward, but he who struggles for righteousness and truth, will have great reward, for even his defeat will be a victory. Self is not a fit vessel to receive any great success; self is small and brittle and its contents will soon be split. Truth, however, is large enough to receive the yearnings and aspirations of all selves and when the selves break like soap-bubbles, their contents will be preserved and in the truth they will lead a life everlasting.

He who goes to battle, O Simha, even though it be in a righteous cause, must be prepared to be slain by his enemies, for that is the destiny of warriors; and should his fate overtake him he has no reason for complaint. But he who is victorious should remember the instability of earthly things. His success may be great, but be it ever so great the wheel of fortune may turn again and bring him down into the dust.

The doctrine of the conquest of self, O Simha, is not taught to destroy the souls of men, but to preserve them. He who has conquered self is more fit to live, to be successful, and to gain victories than he who is the slave of self. He whose mind is free from the illusion of self, will stand and not fall in that battle of life. He whose intentions are righteousness and justice, will meet with no failure, but be successful in his enterprises and his success will endure. He who harbors in his heart love of truth will live and not die, for he has drunk the water of immortality. Struggle then, O general, courageously; and fight your battles vigorously, but be a soldier of truth, and the Tathagata will bless you.

If a man foolishly does me wrong, I will return to him the protection of my ungrudging
love; the more evil comes from him, the more
good shall go from me; the fragrance of goodness
always comes to me, and the harmful air of evil
goes to him. A wicked man who reproaches a
virtuous one is like one who looks up and spits
at heaven; the spittle soils not the heaven, but
comes back and defiles his own person. The
slanderer is like one who flings dust at another
when the wind is contrary; the dust returns on
him who threw it. The virtuous man cannot be
hurt: the misery comes back on the slanderer.

❧ *A celestial deva came to Buddha in the shape of a Brahman whose countenance was bright and whose garments were white like snow. The deva asked questions which the Blessed One answered. The deva said: "What is the sharpest sword? What is the deadliest poison? What is the fiercest fire? What is the darkest night?" Buddha replied:*

A word spoken in wrath is the sharpest sword; covetousness is the deadliest poison; passion is the fiercest fire; ignorance is the darkest night.

The deva said: "Who gains the greatest benefit? Who loses the most benefit? Which armor is invulnerable? What is the best weapon?" Buddha replied:

He is the greatest gainer who gives to others, and he loses most who greedily receives without gratitude. Patience is an invulnerable armor; wisdom is the best weapon.

The deva said: "Who is the most dangerous thief? What is the most precious treasure? Who is most successful in taking away by violence not only on earth, but also in heaven? What is the securest treasure-trove?" Buddha replied:

Evil thought is the most dangerous thief; virtue is the most precious treasure. The mind takes possession of everything not only on earth, but in heaven; immortality is its securest treasure-trove.

The deva said: "What is attractive? What is disgusting? What is the most horrible pain? What is the greatest enjoyment?" Buddha replied:

Good is attractive; evil is disgusting. A bad conscience is the most tormenting pain; deliverance is the height of bliss.

The deva asked: "What causes ruin in the world? What breaks off friendships? What is the most violent fever? Who is the best physician?" Buddha replied:

Ignorance causes the ruin of the world. Envy and selfishness break off friendships. Hatred is the most violent fever, and the Buddha is the best physician.

The deva then asked and said: "Now I have only one doubt to be solved; pray, clear it away: What is it fire can neither burn, nor moisture corrode, nor wind crush down, but is able to reform the whole world?" The Blessed One replied:

Blessing! Neither fire, nor moisture, nor wind can destroy the blessing of a good deed, and blessings reform the whole world.

✄ *A disciple said: "Teach me, O Lord, the meditations to which I must devote myself in order to let my mind enter into the paradise of the pure land." Buddha said:*

There are five meditations. The first meditation is the meditation of love in which you must so adjust your heart that you long for the weal and welfare of all beings, including the happiness of your enemies.

The second meditation is the meditation of pity, in which you think of all beings in distress, vividly representing in your imagination their sorrows and anxieties so as to arouse a deep compassion for them in your soul.

The third meditation is the meditation of joy in which you think of the well-being of others and rejoice with their rejoicings.

The fourth meditation is the meditation on impurity, in which you consider the evil consequences of corruption, the effects of wrongs and evils. How trivial is often the pleasure of the moment and how fatal are its consequences!

The fifth meditation is the meditation on serenity, in which you rise above love and hate, tyranny and thralldom, wealth and want, and regard your own fate with impartial calmness and perfect tranquility.

A true follower of the Tathagata founds not his trust upon austerities or rituals, but giving up the idea of self relies with his whole heart upon Amitabha, the unbounded light of truth.

A disciple said: "Are there no miraculous and wonderful things?" Buddha replied:

Is it not a wonderful thing, mysterious and miraculous to the worldling, that a man who commits wrong can become a saint, that by attaining true enlightenment he will find the path of truth and abandon the evil ways of selfishness? The monk who renounces the transient pleasures of the world for the eternal bliss of holiness, performs the only miracle that can truly be called a miracle. A holy man changes the curses of karma into blessings. But the desire to perform miracles arises either from covetousness or from vanity. Amitabha, the unbounded light, is the source of wisdom, of virtue, of Buddhahood. The deeds of sorcerers and miracle-mongers are frauds, but what is more wondrous, more mysterious, more miraculous than Amitabha?

There was a man born blind, and he said: "I do not believe in the world of light and appearance. There are no colors, bright or somber. There is no sun, no moon, no stars. No one has witnessed these things." His friends remonstrated with him, but he clung to his opinion: "What you say that you see," he objected, "are illusions. If colors existed I should be able to touch them.

They have no substance and are not real. Every-thing real has weight, but I feel no weight where you see colors."

A physician was called to see the blind man. He mixed four simples, and when he applied them to the cataract of the blind man the gray film melted, and his eyes acquired the faculty of sight. The Tathagata is the physician, the cata-ract is the illusion of the thought "I-am," and the four simples are the four noble truths.

When Bhagavat dwelt at Savatthi, he went out with his alms-bowl to beg for food and drew near the house of a Brahman priest while the fire of an offering was blazing upon the altar. The priest said: "Stay there, O wretched samana; thou art an outcast." The Blessed One replied:

Who is an outcast? An outcast is the man who is angry and bears hatred, the man who is wicked and hypocritical, he who embraces error and is full of deceit. Whosoever is a provoker and is avaricious, has evil desires, is envious, wicked, shameless, and without fear to commit wrong, let him be known as an outcast. Not by birth does one become an outcast, not by birth does one become a Brahman; by deeds one becomes an outcast, by deeds one becomes a Brahman.

When I used to enter an assembly, I always became, before I seated myself, in color like unto the color of my audience, and in voice like unto their voice. I spoke to them in their language and then with religious discourse I instructed, quickened, and gladdened them.

My doctrine is like the ocean, having the same eight wonderful qualities. Both the ocean and my doctrine become gradually deeper. Both preserve their identity under all changes. Both cast out dead bodies upon the dry land. As the great rivers, when falling into the main, lose their names and are thenceforth reckoned as the great ocean, so all the castes, having renounced their lineage and entered the Order, become brethren and are reckoned sons of the Perfect One. The ocean is the goal of all streams and of the rain from the clouds, yet is it never overflowing and never emptier: so the Dharma is embraced by many millions of people, yet it neither increases nor decreases. As the great ocean has only one taste, the taste of salt, so my doctrine has only one flavor, the flavor of emancipation. Both the ocean and the Dharma are full of gems and pearls, and both afford a dwelling-place for mighty beings. These are the eight wonderful qualities in which my doctrine resembles the ocean.

◼ *Kutadanta said: "I am told that thou teachest the law, yet thou tearest down religion. And thy disciples despise rites and abandon immolation; but reverence for the gods can be shown only by sacrifices; the very nature of religion consists in worship and sacrifice." Said the Buddha:*

Greater than the immolation of bullocks is the sacrifice of self. He who offers to the gods his evil desires will see the uselessness of slaughtering animals at the altar. Blood has no cleansing power, but the eradiction of lust will make the heart pure. Better than worshiping gods is obedience to the laws of righteousness.

◼ *Kutadanta said: "Thou believest, O Master, that beings are reborn; that they migrate in the evolution of life; and that subject to the law of karma we must reap what we sow. And yet thou teachest the non-existence of the soul! Thy disciples praise utter self-extinction as the highest bliss of Nirvana. If I am merely a compound of sensations and ideas and desires, whither can I go at the dissolution of the body?" Buddha said:*

There is rebirth of character, but no transmigration of a self. Your thought-forms reappear, but there is no ego-entity transferred. The stanza uttered by a teacher is reborn in the scholar who repeats the words. Only through ignorance and delusion do men indulge in the dream that their souls are separate and self-existent entities. Your heart, O Brahman, is cleaving still to self.

I say to you: The Blessed One has not come to teach death, but to teach life, and you discern not the nature of living and dying. This body will be dissolved and no amount of sacrifice will save it. Therefore, seek the life that is of the mind. Where self is, truth cannot be; yet when truth comes, self will disappear. Therefore, let your mind rest in the truth; propagate the truth, put your whole will in it, and let it spread. In the truth you shall live forever. Self is death and truth is life. The cleaving to self is a perpetual dying, while moving in the truth is partaking of Nirvana which is life everlasting.

Then Kutadanta said: "Do I understand thee aright, that Nirvana is not a place, and being no-where it is without reality?" Buddha said:

You do not understand me aright. Tell me, where does the wind dwell? Where does wisdom dwell? Is wisdom a locality? Is there no wisdom, no enlightenment, no righteousness, and no sal-vation, because Nirvana is not a locality? As a great and mighty wind which passes over the world in the heat of the day, so the Tathagata comes to blow over the minds of mankind with the breath of his love, so cool, so sweet, so calm, so delicate; and those tormented by fever assuage their suffering and rejoice at the refreshing breeze.

Said Kutadanta: "Tell me, O Lord, if there be no atman [soul], how can there be immortality?

*Our thoughts are gone when we have done think-
ing." Buddha replied:*

Our thinking is gone, but our thoughts continue. Reasoning ceases, but knowledge remains.
It is as when a man wants, during the night, to
send a letter, and after having his clerk called, has
a lamp lit, and gets the letter written. Then, when
that has been done, he extinguishes the lamp. But
though the writing has been finished and the light
has been put out the letter is still there. Thus does
reasoning cease and knowledge remain; and in the
same way mental activity ceases, but experience,
wisdom, and all the fruits of our acts endure.

*Kutadanta continued: "But tell me O Lord, if
the sankharas [bodily forms] are dissolved, where
is the identity of my self? If my thoughts are
propagated, but my soul migrates, my thoughts
cease to be* my *thoughts and my soul ceases to be*
my *soul." Buddha replied:*

Suppose a man were to light a lamp; is it the
same flame that burns in the first watch of the
night as in the second? Or are there two flames,
one in the first watch and the other in the second
watch? In one sense it is not the same flame,
but in another sense it is the same flame. It burns
the same kind of oil, it emits the same kind of
light, and it serves the same purpose.

Suppose the flame of the first watch had been extinguished during the second watch, would you call it the same if it burns again in the third watch? Has the time that elapsed during the extinction of the flame anything to do with its identity or non-identity? The flame of today is in a certain sense the same as the flame of yesterday, and yet in another sense it is different at every moment. Moreover, the flames of the same kind, illuminating with equal power the same kind of rooms, are in a certain sense the same.

Now, suppose there is a man who feels like you, thinks like you, and acts like you, is he not the same man as you? Do you deny that the same logic holds good for you that holds good for the things of the world?

Kutadanta rejoined slowly: "No, I do not. The same logic holds good universally; but there is a peculiarity about my self which renders it altogether different from everybody else. There may be another man who feels exactly like me, thinks like me, and acts like me; but even if he had the same name he would not be myself." Buddha answered:

True, he would not be you. But tell me, is the person who goes to school one, and that same person when he has finished his schooling another?

Is it one who commits a crime, another who is punished by having his hands and feet cut off? Is sameness constituted by continuity only? Years ago you were a small babe; then a boy; then a youth, and now, you are a man. Is there any identity of the babe and the man? There is an identity in a certain sense only. Indeed there is more identity between the flames of the first and the third watch, even though the lamp might have been extinguished during the second watch. Now which is your true self, that of yesterday, that of today, or that of tomorrow, for the preservation of which you clamor?

It is by a process of evolution that sankharas come to be. There is no sankhara which has sprung into being without a gradual becoming. Your sankharas are the product of your deeds in former existences. The combination of your sankharas is your self. Wheresoever they are impressed thither your self migrates. In your sankharas you will continue to live and you will reap in future existences the harvest sown now and in the past.

"Verily, O Lord," rejoined Kutadanta, "this is not a fair retribution. I cannot recognize the justice that others after me will reap what I am sowing now." Buddha replied:

Is all teaching in vain? Do you not understand that those others are you yourself? You yourself will reap what you sow, not others. Think of a man who is ill-bred and destitute, suffering from the wretchedness of his condition. As a boy he was slothful and indolent, and when he grew up he had not learned a craft to earn a living. Would you say his misery is not the product of his own action, because the adult is no longer the same person as was the boy? I say to you: Not in the heavens, not in the midst of the sea, not if you hide yourself away in the clefts of the mountains, will you find a place where you can escape the fruit of your evil actions. At the same time you are sure to receive the blessings of your good actions. To the man who has long been traveling and who returns home in safety, the welcome of kinfolk, friends, and acquaintances awaits. So, the fruits of his good work bid him welcome who has walked in the path of righteousness, when he finally passes over from the present life into the hereafter.

I have severed all ties because I seek deliverance. How is it possible for me to return to the world? He who seeks religious truth, which is the highest treasure of all, must leave behind all that can concern him or draw away his attention, and must be bent upon that one goal alone. He must free his soul from covetousness and lust, and also from the desire for power.

Indulge in lust but a little, and lust like a child will grow. Wield worldly power and you will be burdened with cares. Better than sovereignty over the earth, better than living in heaven, better than lordship over all the worlds, is the fruit of holiness. I have recognized the illusory nature of wealth and will not take poison as food. Will a fish that has been baited still covet the hook, or an escaped bird love the net? Would a rabbit rescued from the serpent's mouth go back to be devoured? The sick man suffering from fever seeks for a cooling medicine. Shall we advise him to drink that which will increase the fever? Shall we quench a fire by heaping fuel upon it?

✔ People are in bondage, because they have not yet removed the idea of the ego. The thing and its quality are different in our thought, but not in reality. Heat is different from fire in our thought, but you cannot remove heat from fire in reality. You say that you can remove the qualities and leave the thing, but if you think your theory to the end, you will find that this is not so.

Is not man an organism of many aggregates? Are we not composed of various attributes? Man consists of the material form, of sensation, of thought, of dispositions, and, lastly, of under-standing. That which men call the ego when they say "*I* am" is not an entity behind the attributes; it originates by their co-operation.

How much confusion of thought comes from our interest in self, and from our vanity when thinking "*I* am so great," or "*I* have done this wonderful deed?" The thought of your ego stands between your reason and truth; banish it, and then will you see things as they are. He who thinks correctly will rid himself of ignorance and acquire wisdom. The ideas "*I* am," "*I* shall be" or "*I* shall not be" do not occur to a clear thinker.

Moreover, if our ego remains, how can we attain true deliverance? If the ego is to be reborn in any of the three worlds, be it in hell, upon earth, or be it even in heaven, we shall meet again and again the same inevitable doom of sorrow. We shall remain chained to the wheel of individuality and shall be implicated in egotism and wrong. Is this a final escape? All combination is subject to separation, and if we cling to the combination which is the ego, we cannot escape birth, disease, old age, and death.

🔰 Surely if living creatures saw the results of all their evil deeds, they would turn away from them in disgust. But selfhood blinds them, and they cling to their obnoxious desires. They crave pleasure for themselves and they cause pain to others; when death destroys their individuality, they find no peace; their thirst for existence abides and their selfhood reappears in new births. Thus they continue to move in the coil and can find no escape from the hell of their own making. And how empty are their pleasures, how vain are their endeavors! Hollow like the plantain-tree and without contents like the bubble. The world is full of evil and sorrow, because it is full of lust. Men go astray because they think that delusion is better than truth. Rather than truth they follow error, which is pleasant to look at in the beginning but in the end causes anxiety, tribulation, and misery.

🔰 The doctrine of karma is undeniable, but the theory of the ego has no foundation. Like everything else in nature, the life of man is subject to the law of cause and effect. The present reaps what the past has sown, and the future is the product of the present. But there is no evidence of the existence of an immutable ego-being, of a self which remains the same and migrates from body to body. There is rebirth but no transmigration.

Is not this individuality of mine a combination, material as well as mental? Is it not made up of qualities that sprang into being by a gradual evolution? The five roots of sense-perception in this organism have come from ancestors who performed these functions. The ideas which I think, came to me partly from others who thought them, and partly they rise from combinations of the ideas in my own mind. Those who have used the same sense-organs, and have thought the same ideas before I was composed into this individuality of mine, are my previous existences; they are my ancestors as much as the *I* of yesterday is the father of the *I* of today, and the karma of my past deeds affects the fate of my present existence.

🔊 Since it is impossible to escape the results of our deeds, let us practice good works. Let us guard our thoughts that we do no evil, for as we sow so shall we reap. There are ways from light into darkness and from darkness into light. There are ways, also, from the gloom into deeper darkness, and from the dawn into brighter light. The wise use the light they have to receive more light, and advance in the knowledge of truth.

Exhibit true superiority by virtuous conduct and the exercise of reason; meditate deeply on the vanity of earthly things, and understand the fickleness of life. Elevate the mind, and seek sincere faith with firm purpose; transgress not the rules of kingly conduct, and let your happiness depend, not upon eternal things, but upon your own mind. Thus you will lay up a good name for distant ages and will secure the favor of the Teacher.

🖌 There is, O monks, a state where there is neither earth, nor water, nor heat, nor air; neither infinity of space nor infinity of consciousness, nor nothingness, nor perception nor non-perception; neither this world nor that world, neither sun nor moon. It is the uncreate. That I term neither coming nor going nor standing; neither death nor birth. It is without stability, without change; it is the eternal which never originates and never passes away. There is the end of sorrow.

🖌 A man that stands alone, having decided to obey the truth, may be weak and slip back into his old ways. Therefore, stand ye together, assist one another, and strengthen one another's efforts. Be like unto brothers; one in love, one in holi-

ness, and one in your zeal for the truth. Spread
the truth and preach the doctrine in all quarters
of the world, so that in the end all living creatures
will be citizens of the kingdom of righteousness.
This is the holy brotherhood; this is the church,
the congregation of the saints of Buddha; this is
the Order that establishes a communion among
all those who have taken their refuge in Buddha.

Loud is the voice which worldlings make;
but how can they be blamed when divisions arise
also in the Order? Hatred is not appeased in

those who think: "He has reviled me, he has wronged me, he has injured me." For not by hatred is hatred appeased. Hatred is appeased by not-hatred. This is an eternal law.

There are some who do not know the need of self-restraint; if they are quarrelsome we may excuse their behavior. But those who know better, should learn to live in concord. If a man finds a wise friend who lives righteously and is constant in his character, he may live with him, overcoming all dangers, happy and mindful.

But if he finds not a friend who lives righteously and is constant in his character, let him rather walk alone, like a king who leaves his empire and the cares of government behind him to lead a life of retirement like a lonely elephant in the forest. With fools there is no companionship. Rather than to live with men who are selfish, vain, quarrelsome, and obstinate, let a man walk alone.

✄ Though a person be ornamented with jewels, the heart may have conquered the senses. The outward form does not constitute religion or affect the mind. Thus the body of a hermit may wear an ascetic's garb while his mind is immersed in worldliness. A man that dwells in lonely woods and yet covets worldly vanities, is a worldling, while the man in worldly garments may let his heart soar high to heavenly thoughts. There is no distinction between the layman and the hermit, if both have banished the thought of self.

🔔 Truly the body is full of impurity and its end is the charnel house, for it is impermanent and destined to be dissolved into its elements. But being the receptacle of karma, it lies in our power to make it a vessel of truth and not of evil. It is not good to indulge in pleasures of the body, but neither is it good to neglect our bodily needs and to heap filth upon impurities. The lamp that is not cleansed and not filled with oil will be extinguished, and a body that is unkempt, unwashed, and weakened by penance will not be a fit receptacle for the light of truth. Attend to your body and its needs as you would treat a wound which you care for without loving it. Severe rules will not lead the disciples on the middle path which I have taught. Certainly, no one can be prevented from keeping more stringent rules, if he sees fit to do so, but they should not be imposed upon any one, for they are unnecessary.

🔔 A preacher must be full of energy, and cheerful hope, never tiring and never despairing of

55

final success. A preacher must be like a man in quest of water who digs a well in an arid tract of land. So long as he sees that the sand is dry and white, he knows that the water is still far off. But let him not be troubled or give up the task as hopeless. The work of removing the dry sand must be done so that he can dig down deeper into the ground. And often the deeper he has to dig, the cooler and purer and more refreshing will the water be. When after some time of digging he sees that the sand becomes moist, he accepts it as a token that the water is near. So long as the people do not listen to the words of truth, the preacher knows that he has to dig deeper into their hearts; but when they begin to heed his words he apprehends that they will soon attain enlightenment.

The Tathagata is the same unto all beings, differing in his attitude only in so far as all beings are different. The Tathagata recreates the whole world like a cloud shedding its waters without distinction. The great cloud comes up in this wide universe covering all countries and oceans to pour down its rain everywhere, over all grasses, shrubs, herbs, trees of various species, growing on the hills, on the mountains, or in the valleys. Then the grasses, shrubs, herbs, and trees suck the water emitted from that great cloud which is all one essence and has been abundantly poured down; and they will, according to their nature, produce their blossoms and their fruits in season.

Those only who do not believe, call me Gotama, but you call me the Buddha, the Blessed One, the Teacher. And this is right, for I have in this life entered Nirvana, while the life of Gotama has been extinguished. Self has disappeared and the truth has taken its abode in me. This body of mine is Gotama's body and it will be dissolved in due time, and after its dissolution no one, neither God nor man, will see Gotama again. But the truth remains. The Buddha will not die; the Buddha will continue to live in the holy body of the law.

▰ The extinction of the Blessed One will be by that passing away in which nothing remains that could tend to the formation of another self. Nor will it be possible to point out the Blessed One as being here or there. But it will be like a flame in a great body of blazing fire. That flame has ceased; it has vanished and it cannot be said that it is here or there. In the body of the Dharma, however, the Blessed One can be seen; for the Dharma has been preached by the Blessed One.

You are my children, I am your father; through me you have been released from your sufferings. I myself having reached the other shore, help others to cross the stream; I myself having attained salvation, am a savior of others; being comforted, I comfort others and lead them to the place of refuge. I shall fill with joy all the beings whose limbs languish; I shall give happiness to those who are dying from distress; I shall extend to them succor and deliverance.

I was born into the world as the king of truth. The subject on which I meditate is truth. The practice to which I devote myself is truth. The topic of my conversation is truth. My thoughts are always in the truth. For lo! my self has become the truth. Whosoever comprehends the truth will see the Blessed One.

❦ Speak the truth, do not yield to anger; give, if you are asked; by these three steps you will become divine. Let a wise man blow off the impurities of his self, as a smith blows off the impurities of silver, one by one, little by little, and from time to time.

Lead others, not by violence, but by righteousness and equity. He who possesses virtue and intelligence, who is just, speaks the truth, and does what is his own business, him the world will hold dear. As the bee collects nectar and departs without injuring the flower, or its color or scent, so let a sage dwell in the community.

❦ If a traveler does not meet with one who is his better, or his equal, let him firmly keep to his solitary journey; there is no companionship with fools. Long is the night to him who is awake; long is a mile to him who is tired; long is life to the foolish who do not know the true religion. Better than living a hundred years not seeing the highest truth, is one day in the life of a man who sees the highest truth.

❦ The gift of religion exceeds all gifts; the sweetness of religion exceeds all sweetness; the delight in religion exceeds all delights; the extinction of thirst overcomes all pain. Few are there among men who cross the river and reach the goal. The great multitudes are running up and down the shore; but there is no suffering for him who has crossed the river and finished his journey.

⚔ As the lily will grow full of sweet perfume and delight upon a heap of rubbish, thus the disciple of the truly enlightened Buddha shines forth by his wisdom among those who are like rubbish, among the people that walk in darkness. Let us live happily then, not hating those who hate us! Among men who hate us let us dwell free from hatred! Let us live happily then, free from all ailments among the ailing! Let us live happily, then, free from greed among the greedy! Among men who are greedy let us dwell free from greed! The sun is bright by day, the moon shines by night, the warrior is bright in his armor, thinkers are bright in their meditation; but among all, the brightest, with splendor day and night, is the Buddha, the Awakened, the Holy, Blessed.

⚔ When I have passed away and can not longer address you and edify your minds with religious discourse, select from among you men of good family and education to preach the truth in my stead. And let those men be invested with the robes of the Perfect One, let them enter into his abode, and occupy his pulpit.

The robe of the Perfect One is sublime forbearance and patience. His abode is charity and love of all beings. His pulpit is the comprehension of the good law: its eternal truth, and its daily lesson for all men.